Senior
Adult
M I N I S T R Y

Senior Adult
MINISTRY

REGULAR BAPTIST PRESS
1300 North Meacham Road
Schaumburg, Illinois 60173-4888

1994

Acknowledgments

Regular Baptist Press wishes to express appreciation

to the churches

that responded to requests for assistance and data,

to Dr. James T. Dyet,

editor of youth and adult curriculum at RBP, who wrote the
section on the Senior Sunday School class,

and to Scott and Rosanne Byers,

who compiled and edited the manuscript. Mr. Byers is
assistant editor of Sunday School papers at RBP. Mrs. Byers
served RBP as executive secretary for a number of years.

Library of Congress Cataloging-in-Publication Data
Senior adult ministry : a how-to guide for the local church.
     p.   cm. — (RBP service series)
     Includes bibliographical references.
     ISBN 0-87227-184-6
     1. Church work with the aged—Baptists. 2. Christian leadership—
Baptist. I. Series
BV4435.S46 1994
259'.3—dc20   94-28208
                                                      CIP

SENIOR ADULT MINISTRY
© 1994
Regular Baptist Press

Contents

Introduction

The Need for a Senior Ministry

The "graying" of America is underway. Whereas at one time we were an overwhelmingly young population, largely as a result of the post-World War II baby boom, the U.S. is now rapidly becoming a nation of mature people. The fifty-five and over age group is growing three times faster than the national average.[1]

This shift in population is no secret, yet far too few churches are recognizing and responding to it. Targeted evangelistic programs and Christian ministries seem to concentrate on children, the young and upwardly mobile or the single adult. Senior programs in our churches are scarce.

This oversight is unfortunate. The older population in America is a true mission field—not only because the numbers are large but also because the spiritual needs are so great. In a time of shrinking congregations and waning church commitment, this growing group of mature people could be the spark churches are looking for. More than just a fresh crop of pew-sitters, older adults represent an un-tapped labor pool.

A vital church ministry for seniors won't happen on its own. The fact that the number of older people is growing doesn't mean seniors will be knocking down the church doors to get in. Churches must develop a well-thought-out plan for reaching and ministering to seniors. But all the marketing surveys and outreach programs in the world won't do any good if the church doesn't develop a vision—a heart and a burden—for ministering to older people. This needed vision applies not only to seniors in the community at large but also to the ones already within the church walls.

This resource was designed as a reference tool for churches or church leaders seeking to breathe new life into their senior ministries, and for those who are starting a senior ministry from scratch. It is a compilation of material, ideas, thoughts and suggestions gleaned from a Regular Baptist Press survey of churches with active senior ministries. We wish to thank all those churches who took part in the survey.

[1]Win and Charles Arn, *Catch the Age Wave* (Grand Rapids: Baker Book House, 1993), back cover.

PART ONE

Senior Adults: A Profile

We had waited all winter for a warm, sunny day like this one. After six long months of bundling up against the bitter Midwest cold, we were finally free, and we decided this was a perfect day to get outside and explore a nearby state park. People of all ages mingled in the mild April sunshine. Nature lovers watched goldfinches and grosbeaks scramble for seed at the wildlife viewing center feeders; pet owners gave their restless dogs a run; hikers took to the trails. We wanted to try out a trail that led to a suspension bridge spanning the river.

An older friend, Lois, had decided to come along. In spite of the fact that she was in her late 70s, had been recently widowed and faced some nagging health problems, she was determined to have a good time. She kept up a cheerful banter as we ambled down the wooded path.

The trail soon came to a series of steps that wound down the hillside and led toward the suspension bridge. The bridge swung in the breeze, looking a little treacherous. We assured Lois that if she'd like to have a seat and rest for a while, we'd cross the bridge, explore a bit and be back in five or ten minutes.

"What do you mean?" she asked incredulously. "I'm going too!"

So, down the steps we went, Lois tagging along behind us. As we made our way across the bouncing, swinging, suspension bridge, we were feeling rather daring—until we met a large group of senior adults coming *back* from a hike!

"Lois," I remarked, "old people sure aren't what they used to be!"

CHAPTER 1

Who Seniors Are

The senior adult population in the United States *is* changing. *The Second 50 Years* maintains that today thousands of people live to be past 100, and most have the potential to live to be 115.[1] Due perhaps to better nutrition and health care, people are just plain living longer. *The Statistical Bulletin* reports, "Expectation of life at birth in the United States rose to a record high of 75.7 years in 1992."[2] The U.S. Census Bureau predicts newborn life expectancy will soon reach 82 years.[3] All this has resulted in a booming population of older people in our society.

Not only are people living longer these days, they are *enjoying* living longer. Longer life expectancies translate into better health and vigor enjoyed by older people. Today's seniors have realized that retirement doesn't necessarily mean the rocking chair. Many love to travel, sightsee, exercise, have fun, make new friends and do all the things they were too busy to do when they were working.

The concept of retirement, too, has undergone a change. In years past, most people considered their retirement as a time to play or to be "put out to pasture," an end to their days as a valuable member of society. But modern seniors rebel against this outdated idea. They want to remain useful; to continue learning and growing personally; to remain viable and valuable members of their families, communities and churches.

Their Differences

We must understand that when we refer to "seniors," we are referring to an incredibly disparate group. Contrary to popular opinion, seniors are not all the same. The senior adult years span a wide age range, from newly retired (50s to 60s) to age 100 and up. This means people with an age difference of forty to fifty years are grouped in the same age bracket! Within this broad range are small subgroups, each with its own particular characteristics and needs. A senior may be a married, newly retired businessman with young-adult children; a fragile 90-year-old, widowed shut-in; or an active bachelor in his 70s.

If you're still not convinced that the over-55 age group is diverse, consider this startling demographic statistic: In two years, the baby boom generation—more than 77 million strong—turns 50! It's hard to imagine what that group will have in common with people who lived during the Great Depression.

The point is, seniors are not stereotypes—they are people with distinct personalities, opinions, experiences and abilities.

Their Struggles

Change has been a constant companion during the lives of older people. They have, literally, been through it all. They have been married, raised a family and seen their children grow up and leave home; they have experienced retirement from their jobs or careers, relocation, death of a spouse or friends and lifestyle changes brought about by failing health or finances.

Most seniors have negotiated at least an uneasy peace with change, having learned to accept it as part and parcel of life. Yet they still must deal with the many conflicts that change brings to their lives. They face a unique set of struggles.

Health

An uncertain future looms ahead of most seniors, regardless of their age bracket. Although many of them, especially the younger ones, are strong, active, healthy people, they still are forced to face the reality that their bodies are deteriorating. They no longer feel as physically strong and vigorous as they used to feel. Some of them must even depend (albeit reluctantly) on family members or friends to meet their physical needs.

The older years bring a whole new set of health-related questions for seniors. What if I become seriously ill? Will I have to live in a nursing home? What about death? Will it be painful? Will I lose any of my physical or mental capabilities?

Will I lose my spouse? Will I become a burden to my children? What about health care? Will I be cared for? Will I understand all the health insurance forms I need to fill out?

Loneliness

Loneliness, a sad factor of life in our mobile society, is especially prevalent among seniors. Children grow up, go away to college and take jobs in faraway cities. It is a rare family that has members of more than two generations living in the same town or city.

Many seniors are lonely because they've lost their spouse—the person with whom they shared everything: money and possessions, children, a home, good times and bad—their very lives. The loss of a mate of four or five decades leaves an incredible void and requires significant lifestyle adjustment. Seniors have also lost family members and friends. And for those who never married, being old and living alone can be a pitiable existence. As human supports crumble, the senior adult needs somewhere to turn for comfort and help.

Retirement

Retirement is a significant milestone in life; it is both an ending and a beginning. Retirement marks the end of a lifelong vocation or career and the official beginning of life as a "senior citizen" (a label most seniors despise).

New retirees are often surprised at how much their job or career defined who they are. Upon retirement, their world suddenly seems aimless and unstructured. Work is more than just a source of a steady paycheck: it is a valuable social institution because it gives structure to life. It provides self-esteem and a network of social relationships, insures a regular income and automatically defines a daily routine.

The new retiree has many adjustments to make. Most undergo a feeling of loss, much like grief over a lost loved one. They may feel that their life's goals are now complete, that they've reached the top rung of the ladder and there's nothing left to accomplish. They must adjust to changes in routine, such as not going to work every morning or learning to live with a spouse 24 hours a day.

If a senior is forced by his employer to retire, or if retirement is financially impossible, he may find himself forced back into a highly competitive job market that seldom views age as an asset. Such seniors must update their résumés and their job skills.

Financial Pressures

Older people face a myriad of financial pressures too. While many have worked hard, invested wisely and become financially secure, others, especially widows and the very old, must struggle to get by on fixed incomes. They must learn to depend on an undependable government for their Social Security checks. An unfortunate few must even rely on the kindness of family, friends and the church to eke out a meager existence.

Many younger seniors seem caught in the middle; their financial responsibilities bridge the gap between young and old. Forced to support not only their children but also their parents, they write checks monthly for both college tuition and nursing-home care.

Another surprisingly common social trend is for the grandparents to care for their grandchildren because the children's parents are either unwed or divorced and the mother must work outside the home. This responsibility places undue financial and emotional strain on the grandparents.

Seniors of all ages and income brackets face financial questions: Will I have enough money to live on? Will my investments remain sound? When can I draw on retirement money without penalty? Will I still be able to help my family out financially if they need it? Will health insurance pay my bills if I become hospitalized?

[1]Walter J. Cheney, William J. Diehm, Franke Seeley. *The Second Fifty Years* (New York: Paragon House, 1992), p. 260.

[2]*The Statistical Bulletin*, Vol. 74, No. 3; July–September 1993. Published by Metropolitan Life Insurance Company, p. 28.

[3]U.S. Bureau of the Census, *Current Population Reports, Series P-25, No. 1092.* "Population projections of the U.S. by age, sex, race, and Hispanic origin: 1992 to 2050." Washington, D.C. Nov., 1992.

CHAPTER 2

A Biblical Approach

In Bible times, life was pretty much the same for a young person as it had been for his father, his grandfather, his great-grandfather—on and on for generations. The apostle Paul lived in a world that was not much different technologically from the one Moses lived in.

Western society is much different. Our culture is not one of harmonious continuity from generation to generation, but rather one of harsh and abrupt change. Since the end of

World War II, American society has been changing at a breathtaking speed. The world that a teen of the 1990s lives in bears little resemblance to the Depression-era world his great-grandfather knew. This rapid change has fragmented the age groups in our society.

The change in our culture has been driven largely by the change in technology. New technology arises almost overnight, and only people who can adapt to the new survive in the marketplace. This trend has produced an inordinately high regard for the aggressive vitality of youth over the staid, solid wisdom of age—so much so that people try to hide that they're aging with face-lifts and wrinkle creams. Individuals who are too obviously old are hidden away in nursing homes and institutions. "Older persons," reports Charles Sell, "are forced out of the mainstream of life to become part of an ignored and depreciated minority group."[1]

The Second 50 Years reports an alarming statistic: "Today, the greatest proportion of suicides are among the elderly."[2] This fact is shocking enough on its own, but it is doubly so because it is so unrecognized. Teen suicide gets wide attention and public funding, but senior suicide goes unreported. It is stark proof of the overwhelming needs that exist within the senior adult population.

The downward slide in respect for older people may run rampant in American society, and even in our churches, but it is counter to what the Word of God teaches. Consider the following Scripture principles and passages.

Scriptural Value of Old Age

Old Age Is Good

"And thou shalt go to thy fathers in peace; thou shalt be buried in a good old age" (Gen. 15:15).

"Then Abraham gave up the ghost, and died in a good old age, an old man, and full of years . . ." (Gen. 25:8).

"And Gideon the son of Joash died in a good old age . . . " (Judg. 8:32).

Old Age Is Respectable

"Thou shalt rise up before the hoary head, and honour the face of the old man" (Lev. 19:32).

"What knowest thou, that we know not? what understandest thou, which is not in us? With us are both the gray headed and very aged men" (Job 15:9, 10).

"Hearken unto thy father that begat thee, and despise not thy mother when she is old" (Prov. 23:22).

"Rebuke not an elder, but intreat him as a father; and the younger men as brethren; the elder women as mothers" (1 Tim. 5:1, 2).

Old Age Has Blessings All Its Own

"And the women said unto Naomi, Blessed be the LORD, which hath not left thee this day without a kinsman, that his name may be famous in Israel. And he shall be unto thee a restorer of thy life, and a nourisher of thine old age . . . " (Ruth 4:14, 15).

"Children's children are the crown of old men . . . " (Prov. 17:6a).

Old Age Is Wise

"Remember the days of old, consider the years of many generations: ask thy father, and he will shew thee; thy elders, and they will tell thee" (Deut. 32:7).

"And king Rehoboam consulted with the old men. . . . But he forsook the counsel of the old men . . ." (1 Kings 12:6, 8). "And Israel rebelled against the house of David" (2 Chron. 10:19).

Some Biblical Examples

Abraham and Sarah had longed for a child their whole lives, but they found themselves old and still childless. Should they give up hope or continue to believe God despite the seemingly impossible physical circumstances? Scripture tells us that Abraham "staggered not at the promise of God" (Rom. 4:20). And Sarah "delivered of a child when she was past age, because she judged him faithful who had promised" (Heb. 11:11).

Likewise, Zacharias and Elisabeth dealt with the heartache of barrenness. But God had a surprise for them in their senior years. Elizabeth "conceived a son in her old age" (Luke 1:36). God doesn't desert people just because they're old. He still uses and rewards them.

Consider Caleb, who stood strong for God but never received the recognition Joshua did. However, he remained faithful. And at the age of 85, his faith and physical strength were just as vital and vigorous as the day that Moses had sent him to spy out the land of Canaan (Josh. 14:10–12).

Anna was deprived of her husband early in life, yet she did not grow bitter. Rather, she chose to devote her life in service to her God, serving Him "with fastings and prayers night and day" (Luke 2:37). God rewarded Anna's faith with a special glimpse of the promised Messiah.

---

[1]Charles M. Sell. *Transition* (Chicago: Moody Press, 1985), p. 196.

[2]*The Second Fifty Years*, p. 368.

PART TWO

Seniors in the Church

CHAPTER 3

A Closer Look

How should the local church respond to the growing population of older people in society and to that age group's pressing spiritual needs? What obligations does the church have toward older people?

First, the local church has a responsibility to evangelize them. Jesus commanded Christians to preach the gospel to "every creature" (Mark 16:15). "Target evangelism," concentrating evangelistic efforts on a particular social group, has become a buzzword in church circles these days. Unfortunately, most efforts at target evangelism focus on children, teens, baby boomers or yuppies. Seniors have, for the most part, been ignored.

But the older segment of society needs the gospel as much as the younger. In fact, they probably are more receptive to it. While seniors don't sit at home brooding about the day of their death, most have at least confronted it as a reality. This fact, coupled with the struggles seniors face, makes older people more attuned to the spiritual side of life and may spur them to question non-Christian views of life and death that they've held throughout their lives.

But in another sense, the older population may be more difficult to *reach* with the gospel. More than any other age group, seniors have been heavily "churched." As compared to younger people, an overwhelming percentage of older people have been to church—of one sort or another. They grew up in an era when going to church was just something most people did. At the very least, church membership was a sign of social respectability. As a result, when it comes to spiritual matters, older people may tend to think they've "heard it all before." An effective senior ministry must consider the implications of this attitude and not offer seniors more clichés or spiritual pabulum. Seniors need the Bible's real answers to their real problems.

Second, the church can be a support network for believing seniors. The local church has a duty to provide spiritual support for all Christians, young and old (Gal. 6:2). Where else can seniors find encouragement and hope? Where else can they receive close Christian fellowship and opportunities to worship and serve the Lord? The church is the one group seniors are *not* expected to retire from.

Third, the church must rethink its view of seniors and

realign it with Scripture. The trend of Western society to put older people on the shelf, to view them as useless antiquities, is not only counterproductive; it's unscriptural. At the risk of sounding politically correct, this sort of attitude amounts to ageism, the practice of treating older people as if they're less valuable simply because of their age. Win and Charles Arn write, "If the church is going to seize the opportunity of effectively ministering to senior adults, it will need to root out the ageism found in subtle ways in so many congregations."[1]

For example, when someone is needed to serve on the missions committee or to help with decorations for the spring banquet, do you consider any seniors? Do all the positions of leadership and responsibility go to the young and aggressive? Are seniors given an opportunity to serve the Lord in the church? And ageism doesn't have to be intentional or overt to be damaging. It can be merely overlooking the talents and experience of senior adults, somehow thinking that their age makes them less qualified.

Setting Goals

You'd never think of embarking on a long trip without a destination or a road map. Producing an effective senior ministry in the church is no different. A clearly stated goal gives direction to our efforts, tells us what we want to accomplish and how we are to get there. Without goals, any undertaking, no matter how sincere we are, will flounder aimlessly. Here are seven suggested goals for a senior ministry:

• to reach older adults with the gospel of Jesus Christ;

• to increase the local church body's awareness of and concern for its older members;

• to provide seniors with Biblical answers to their problems;

• to promote among seniors spiritual growth and dependence on God for comfort and peace;

• to promote the church's full utilization of the skills and abilities of seniors;

• to fully integrate seniors into the church body to make them as much a part of the church as younger members;

• to provide seniors with opportunities to fellowship with one another.

Ministering to Seniors

If the church is to develop an effective ministry to older people, it must focus on three key concepts: integrating seniors, involving them and finding practical ways to help them.

Integrate Them

When targeting any specific age group for ministry, we walk a fine line between meeting the needs of the group and isolating it. In its ministry to seniors, the church should avoid creating a group of older people who are somehow seen as separate from the rest of the church body. We don't want to base a senior ministry on the fact that seniors are different from the rest of the church body. Unfortunately, the isolation of age groups is generally the norm in many churches already—the teens hang around with other teens, the young marrieds fellowship with other young marrieds, and so on up the age ladder.

We must never forget that all age groups are honorable and valuable in the sight of God. Scripture teaches us that *all* parts of the Body of Christ have value simply because they are who God created them to be. Each member has a function that no other body part should attempt to perform (1 Cor. 12:25–27). These verses apply as much to age groups as they do to talents and spiritual gifts. No age group is any more, or any less, important than another.

The Bible also teaches that all Christians, young and old alike, are members of the same family—God's family. And who ever heard of a family that tried to keep people of different age groups separate? What family keeps the grandparents separate from the children and the children from their parents? The unity of the Body *is* a precious thing.

The trick is to meet the needs of the older church members while making them feel as much a part of the church as the younger members. The best way to accomplish this goal is to increase interaction between age groups. Where there is interaction, there is communication, and communication is a step toward unity. The more the members of a church interact with one another, the more unified it can become. As Paul encouraged the church at Ephesus, "Endeavouring to keep the unity of the Spirit in the bond of peace" (Eph. 4:3).

Here are some practical ideas to promote the integration of seniors into the church body:

• Feature special music by mixed groups of seniors and young church members, even children.

• Feature one senior adult or couple each month. Have them give their testimonies in church and set up a display portraying the highlights of their lives. This exposure promotes interaction by familiarizing the other church members with the seniors, and it provides conversation starters. It may even help a younger church member identify with a senior by seeing common interests, problems or struggles.

• Set up a program in which high school students work for the seniors (mowing lawns, weeding or painting, for instance) and then the seniors, in return, provide refreshments for the high school socials.

• Let your senior adults be grandparents for a day and

take grandchildren (either theirs or "adopted") to the zoo, a ball game or some other function. You may wish to include parents so the kids won't be afraid to be alone with someone they hardly know.

• Involve children in visiting shut-ins. This activity conveys to children the importance of older people and helps them see the worth of all persons—even those who are dependent upon others.

• Have the teen group sponsor a dinner or other social for the seniors.

• Organize a talent night involving the whole church, and use this time to promote the seniors' talents.

• Begin a secret pal program between the teens and the senior adults.

• Involve the whole church in volunteer teams to help older seniors: transportation to church services, home repairs, yard work, transportation to doctor's visits, and so on. Be sensitive to the fact that younger seniors may take such an offer as an insinuation that they can no longer care for themselves.

• Organize a senior adult choir to sing periodically in church.

• Let the seniors sponsor a fellowship after the evening service. One senior group set up a display of their crafts, served light refreshments and invited the church to come and browse. Such an activity stimulates interaction between the age groups by providing an opportunity for the younger generation to observe the skills of the older people.

Involve Them

The second aspect of senior ministry goes hand-in-hand with the first: involve your seniors! One of the best ways to make someone feel valuable is to put him to work. Older people are no exception. Use them in the work of the church whenever possible. This sounds like a trite suggestion, but seniors are often overlooked simply because they're older. Too many church leaders forget that older church members have wisdom, skills, abilities and years of rich experience. Seniors are a largely untapped resource within the local church.

Ageism in the church may be due in some part to the trend of professionalism that has crept into the ministry lately. The leaders, the trained professionals, perform, while the untrained spectators sit and watch. This mind-set is destructive to the unity of the entire church, but seniors suffer the brunt of it. Older people may be slow, hard of hearing or weak of voice—an on-stage embarrassment to the professional.

This observation is not to recommend that the church sacrifice the integrity or quality of its pulpit ministry merely to stroke the egos of a few older members. First Peter 4:11 stresses the idea of using people within their strengths—"If any man minister, let him do it as of the ability which God giveth: that God in all things may be glorified through Jesus Christ. . . ." It makes no sense to let a senior lead the singing if he has no musical ability or to teach a class if he can't speak in public. What church leaders can do is keep their eyes open for the talents older church members have and remember to use them when the opportunity arises. Seniors have a duty to serve Christ, just as younger people do. Christ never intended for them to sit and collect dust in the pews.

What can older church members do? They can perform many of the tasks younger ones can do. As with other positions within the church, it depends on where their strengths lie. Seniors can

• listen to children recite Bible verses in Awana or Bible clubs;

- teach a Sunday School class;
- lead the singing or the choir;
- organize and schedule special music;
- cut out visuals for teaching ministries;
- participate in missionary committees or write missionary letters (especially good for shut-ins);
- compile a church history and maintain it;
- assist in church remodeling (even if physical work is beyond their capabilities, they may supervise projects in which they have expertise and experience: the women may supervise cleaning or reupholstery; the men may supervise painting, carpet-laying or concrete cleaning);
- make sets for church drama productions;
- present a special story time in children's church;
- help in the church mail room (collate church newspaper or other bulletin inserts, label and stuff church mailings);
- present special music;
- separate Sunday School take-home paper packs for separate Sundays;
- pray (*not* a lesser ministry!).

Seniors can also help out in less concrete ways. They can encourage younger church members by being a living example of perseverance in the Christian life. They can communicate the value of having a rich family heritage by sharing their knowledge of the past. They can model respect and dignity. They can lend a listening ear or share their acquired wisdom. They can be an example of contentment. They can be a powerful testimony of Christ's faithfulness. The church can only benefit by utilizing this immense resource.

Help Them in Practical Ways

When Christ was on earth, He understood the close connection between the physical and the spiritual needs of people. He healed the sick, comforted the mourning and fed the hungry. This ministry often opened a window of opportunity for Him to discuss with people their spiritual needs. In much the same way, the church can better minister to seniors if it is sensitive to their physical needs. A local church might

• adapt church facilities to the specialized needs of seniors adults with regard to acoustics, building accessibility, lighting, rest rooms and ventilation;

• provide special parking slots for seniors near the church entrance;

• provide transportation—not only to church services and senior adult activities, but also to medical appointments, drug stores and grocery stores;

• provide shut-ins with opportunities for Bible study, worship and fellowship;

• make large-print Bibles and hymnals available in churches;

• be familiar with public services available to the aging in order to provide helpful information to those in need;

• establish an active shut-in visitation program.

It is important not to make such physical aids too conspicuous. In other words, don't advertise seniors' physical limitations. They face an uphill battle in overcoming stereotypical views as it is. Younger seniors, especially, may resent the idea that they're hard of hearing or unable to fend for themselves. As in everything else, seek a balanced approach.

Tips for Pastors

More than perhaps any other person in the church, the pastor can promote the cause of senior ministry. As the church's spiritual leader, he can help the congregation cultivate an attitude of love and respect for seniors. He can include topics that concern seniors in his sermons, for instance.

Speaking about older church members with an attitude of respect helps too. (Never make "old age" jokes, for instance.) Most of all, if the pastor shows a willingness to use seniors in his ministry, the rest of the church will tend to view seniors in a better light.

Using the Church Library

Even something as ordinary as the church library can be employed to enhance your senior ministry. You could, for instance, circulate books to shut-ins. Or set aside a library section solely for books, magazines and video and audio tapes of interest to seniors. Other than Biblical materials, seniors like Christian books about grandparenting, retirement, parent care, aging and so on. And don't forget to include a collection of large-print books and Bibles.

---

[1]Win and Charles Arn, *Catch the Age Wave* (Grand Rapids: Baker Book House, 1993), p. 55.

CHAPTER 4

The Sunday School Class

The linchpin of the church's ministry to seniors is the Sunday School. Other activity groups for older adults have their place and may even be necessary for a complete ministry, but a strong Sunday School class is irreplaceable.

The Sunday School performs several important functions. It supplies the Biblical and spiritual training seniors need to face life's challenges; it acts as a place for seniors to bring their peers to hear the gospel; it forms a base for leadership for a senior adult group and supplies a vital core group of believers on which to base other senior ministries.

Organizing the Class

The definition of a senior varies, depending on who you ask. If you've read a "senior citizen" coupon lately, you've noticed that the definition of a senior is anyone "over 55." This definition is in keeping with the trend toward retiring early, before age 65. These "young" seniors are at a very different stage in life than their older senior class members.

In order to meet the spiritual needs of both younger and older seniors successfully, it may be necessary to divide the group. One class could be comprised of people between the ages of 55 and 70, for instance; the other class might consist of people over 70.

But careful evaluation is necessary here. Do you really have enough seniors to form two Sunday School classes? Is there adequate leadership for two classes, three classes or even more? And before you take any steps, identify the seniors' needs. Would they benefit from being divided into two or more groups? Or would they resent being compartmentalized?

Even if the class is divided as described, great disparity between class members will still exist. Sitting side by side in the younger class could be a 55-year-old, newly retired professional couple and a 70-year-old widowed homemaker. In the older class you could have an energetic 75-year-old and a barely ambulatory widower in his 90s. If you don't divide the group at all, the differences are even more stark.

It may be necessary to end the "senior" category at some age—say 80 or 90—at which a new category, "the elderly," takes over. The needs of the two groups are that different. It's hard to merge a ministry to active retired people and feeble elderly.

But we must stress here that intergenerational fellowship and learning can still take place in classes of mixed ages—even groups having young, middle and older adults. Separating older adults from younger adults may fragment the church's fellowship instead of building it and destroy your efforts to integrate seniors into the church body. The church leadership should introduce a new senior adult Sunday School class only with the seniors' input and enthusiastic goodwill.

Teaching Methods

It's a common misconception that seniors either can't learn or don't need to learn. They *can* learn, and there are Biblical truths and spiritual principles they still have to internalize. No one ever reaches a point in his Christian life when he has "arrived," when he knows it all.

Even "well-churched" seniors can benefit from a Sunday School lesson—it all depends on the relevancy of the material. The senior Sunday School curriculum should be chosen with this fact in mind. If the curriculum is applicable to the lives of older people, they will learn and spiritually benefit from it.

One way to make sure that the Sunday School lesson material is relevant to the lives of older people is to let them have some input in choosing it. While the leadership of the church should not abandon its supervisory role and let the class run itself, leaders should at least listen to the students' ideas, preferences and concerns. This input will ensure that the lesson material chosen is relevant to older people's interests and spiritual needs.

The teacher of the senior Sunday School class must be able to relate to older people and be sensitive to their needs without patronizing them. This prerequisite nearly mandates that the teacher be an older person. It's hard to imagine a 30-year-old lecturing people twice his age on remaining true to Christ during the latter years or some other topic relevant only to seniors.

Whatever his age, the teacher should have enthusiasm. Someone has said that nothing is as contagious as enthusiasm—or the lack thereof! No one likes a boring class, not even seniors. They respond heartily to a teaching approach that is relevant and interesting and that involves them in the lesson.

The Regular Baptist Press adult Sunday School curriculum lends itself easily to the senior class. The adult teacher's manual includes a Student Needs section describing the truths that different adult age groups—younger, middle and older—should glean from the lesson. The teaching methods and discussion questions often include ideas and strategies to help the teacher tailor the lesson to the particular age group of his students. (For more information about ordering Regular Baptist Press Sunday School curriculum, call the toll-free order line at 1-800-727-4440.)

Meeting Needs in the Class Session

Like other adults, seniors have basic emotional needs. In some respects, those needs may be more pronounced because their circle of friends is shrinking and their range of interests and activities is diminishing. They need to feel accepted, loved, secure and useful. The teacher who simply lectures to his seniors in every Sunday School class session may not be meeting those critical needs. However, by employing the teaching methods provided in each Regular Baptist Press adult teacher's manual, he can help meet seniors' needs while sparking and sustaining their interest in learning how the Bible relates to the "fall and winter" years of life.

The RBP adult teacher's manual frequently suggests small group discussion. When seniors are allowed to discuss in a supportive atmosphere how Scripture relates to a life issue, they accept one another unconditionally. Christian fellowship develops as several seniors in a group share their concerns, experiences, insights and Biblical principles. In the small group, the dynamics of Christian love come into play. Individuals feel free to ask questions or to offer helpful comments. Someone might say, "John, I think I know how you feel. I've been there." Another person might suggest, "Mary, I know how lonely a Saturday afternoon can be. Why don't a few of us meet at the mall for lunch, then do some serious shopping?" Perhaps someone else will suggest practical ways to stretch a limited income while trusting God to meet every need.

The use of overhead transparencies, provided in the RBP teaching packet and shown in the teacher's manual, can help seniors capture and remember important Bible truths. Like every group of students, seniors learn better when visuals accompany the spoken word. And the better they learn, the greater their sense of accomplishment grows.

Senior adults possess enormous skills. Some have acting ability; others write clearly and persuasively. Some are artistic; others excel in public speaking. Appreciating this diversity, RBP builds into adult teacher's manuals opportunities for seniors to put those skills to work in class sessions. A sense of accomplishment grows as seniors express Bible truths in poetry, write words to accompany a hymn or chorus, create bumper-sticker Christian messages, perform in skits, role-play, lead a discussion or present a report.

As adults interact and minister to one another, they develop a sense of belonging. They perceive themselves as members of a caring group of believers. They feel secure and loved. As they contribute to the success of each Sunday School class session, they experience a sense of accomplishment. They perceive Sunday School as a place where they can relate to others and grow spiritually. Convinced that Sunday School meets needs, seniors feel comfortable in inviting their friends to join them for one of the most exciting and profitable hours of the week.

Keeping in Touch

To keep the Sunday School class alive and thriving, its members must actively communicate with each other. This communication promotes unity and prevents the group from becoming fragmented—one of the goals of a senior ministry.

When people start to drift away from church, one of the first things they begin to skip is Sunday School. Open communication between class members can keep this drifting from happening or can at least let absentees know they are missed.

Here are some further suggestions to help keep your Sunday School class in touch:

• Set up a phone committee to call every class member regularly to check on health, remind about meetings and activities, and get prayer requests. Shut-ins, especially, may enjoy helping out with this detail.

• Send welcome notes to people who have visited the class.

• Send birthday and get-well cards to members.

• Visit members in the hospital.

• Provide support for members in crisis: telephone calls, notes, meals.

• Mail or hand-deliver church bulletins or Wednesday night prayer bulletins to shut-ins each week.

• Set up a Sunday School program for shut-ins. Volunteers can take notes in class, then "teach" the lesson to the shut-in during the week. This class helps the shut-ins be fed spiritually, and it also helps them stay abreast of what is going on in church.

PART THREE

Senior Adult Groups

Much of the material for this chapter was derived from a Regular Baptist Press survey of senior adult ministries in GARBC churches around the country.

Once you have established a solid senior Sunday School class, you may consider expanding your church's ministry to older people. A senior adult group that meets during the week for service, outreach, prayer, fellowship and fun may be the key to developing a complete senior ministry in your church.

But remember that while your senior group should provide its members opportunities for fun and socializing, its major goal should always be Christian service. In other words, if you focus on good times, your group will run the risk of degenerating into nothing more than a social club. Keep your group's compass set on serving Christ, and the good times will follow naturally.

CHAPTER 5

Getting Started

Ilf you have a solid group of older Christians in your Sunday School, you have a good foundation for a senior adult group. Those seniors probably will be interested in forming a group that will give them both an outlet for their abilities and opportunities to get together regularly.

Objectives

Just like the senior ministry as a whole, the senior adult group should be based on concrete, carefully thought-out goals. Here is a list of possible group objectives:

- to promote the evangelism of older adults by their peers;
- to help seniors grow spiritually, emotionally and intellectually;
- to provide opportunities for fun, fellowship and social activities;
- to provide spiritual accountability among seniors;
- to give seniors a base of operation for expanding their service to the church and to the community at large.

A statement of purpose goes hand-in-hand with the setting of goals. A clear-cut statement gives the group direction and lets everyone know what the group wishes to accomplish. It encapsulates the broad goals you may have made and puts them in a form that's easily communicated. Win and Charles Arn, in their book *Catch the Age Wave*, suggest the following statement:

> The _____ group has as its purpose to serve, not to be served. We believe God is calling us to take his love in concrete ways to the unchurched senior adults in our community, as well as to extend the love of God and the love of the family of God to those within the church. These goals will be accomplished through regular planned activities and emphases, with the anticipated result of God's blessing and people coming to Christ and the church. By-products of these activities will be spiritual growth, *koinonia*, social and recreational development.[1]

The Groundwork

Just like sowing a crop, the first step, breaking ground, is the hardest. But it is also the most important. Getting your senior group off on a good foot with the church leadership is crucial. The need for a senior group, as well as the purpose of the ministry and the commitment it will entail, should be explained. Enlist the leadership's understanding and support.

It will probably be necessary to appoint a committee that will get the ball rolling. The committee will most likely be made up of senior members of the Sunday School along with members of the church staff and administration. It is a good idea to include a representative from each church ministry (e.g., visitation, library) in the planning group, because as they become more familiar with the seniors, they'll rely on them more for filling church-ministry needs. This involvement will also aid coordination of the total church ministries.

Some churches have discovered the usefulness of surveys when starting a senior group. These surveys poll the seniors in the Sunday School to help the leadership determine the seniors' needs and wants regarding a senior adult group.

Several surveys are available for use within your church. *How to Minister to Senior Adults in Your Church* by Horace L. Kerr (Broadman Press) and the *Senior Adult Leader's Notebook* compiled by W. L. Howse III (Convention Press) both contain useful surveys. You may also consider creating your own survey. List the ministries and activities the church could provide for the group, and then let the seniors rate them according to their needs. Also list service opportunities the group will provide for seniors, and have members indicate the areas they'd be willing to help in.

After the survey results have been analyzed, the next step is to decide on a time and place for regular meetings and determine a basic format. Electing or appointing group officers and giving them clearly written job descriptions will simplify the logistical coordination necessary for a smoothly running group. Don't forget the need for good secretarial support to maintain accurate records and to deal congenially with people.

Check to see if the church can provide financial help to start the senior adult group, but remember that financial independence is a worthy goal. It helps the group members feel that they are in control of their group and can pay their own way.

Be organized and consistent in your planning, but remember that every church and senior adult group is different. Don't expect an idea that worked for one church to work automatically for your group. Every group's needs and assets are different—use what you have.

Leadership

The senior group leader must be someone both the pastor and the congregation trust. He should be sensitive to the needs of older people, have a desire to work with them and be available to them. He must listen to the seniors' input, delegate appropriately and then support those with whom he has shared responsibility. The leader must emphasize that he is not there to tell the group what to do, but is merely the coordinator, or at the most, the "chief coordinator."

If your church has only one senior adult Sunday School class, consider continuing the class leadership structure over into the senior adult group. But if your church has more than one class, you may want to choose a separate leader for the senior adult group. However, keep in mind that coordination between the Sunday School class and the senior adult group is imperative in all areas.

If the group leader is in the older age bracket (over 70), the group may tend to attract only older seniors. Having younger adult seniors assisting him will help bring in the younger set.

Our survey revealed several leadership approaches that are used by churches with active senior ministries.

Church Staff Member

This person may be either full-time or part-time, but he is a part of the paid church staff. The majority of senior adult leaders surveyed are in this category. Some have additional responsibilities besides the senior adult group. Their titles are as follows: adult ministries counselor, associate pastor of pastoral care, pastor of senior adults, discipleship and counseling director, senior ministries director.

The Pastor

Of the senior adult groups we surveyed, only one in twenty is led by the pastor. In one situation, the pastor himself is a senior but is assisted by a younger adult. The senior group in this church has had a successful outreach ministry for years and is alive and growing.

Younger Couples

Directing a senior group is a definite challenge for younger people. They usually need to earn the group's trust and respect by listening to seniors' input and implementing many of their ideas. But if the class will accept them, younger adults can breathe life into a stale program; they bring vigor, enthusiasm and new ideas to the group. It is interesting to note that even groups with older leadership often involve younger adults in the planning process.

Elected Officers

Under this arrangement, the pastor or Sunday School teacher may offer counsel and ideas, but the main leadership responsibility comes from within the group itself. The group elects officers from within the group to fulfill written job descriptions for a one-year period. The job descriptions include the qualifications and requirements of the job. These officers may form a committee of from four to ten people.

Planning

Whether the group has officers, a paid staff leader or volunteer help, planning always enhances its success. The following planning tips may be helpful:

• Plan a year ahead, coordinating all dates with the church calendar. Announce tentative dates so the group can keep them open. For example: "The fall banquet will be either the second or third weekend of October."

• Involve as many members of your group as possible in the planning process. When people are involved in the decision-making process, it becomes *their* group. For example, plan a day trip to a particular destination, then list available options at that particular location. It might be a string quartet concert in the park, a Victorian home tour or an orchid nursery tour. Let the group members vote on what they want to do.

• Get ideas from the group and then schedule as many of those ideas as you can during the year. Constantly get feedback. After an activity, ask the group members what they thought about it. But remember, if you ask for their input, make sure you use it!

Naming the Group

The name "Senior Adults" is popular since it is widely understood and accepted. Some groups merely call themselves "Seniors." One of the groups interviewed reported that they used to be known as "Keenagers," but the younger seniors weren't attracted to this "older image." They now call their group the "Adult Fellowship."

But many senior groups take a more creative approach to

naming their group. Although caution needs to be used with cute titles, many seniors do find it fun to have a special name. Some of the names we ran across are Go Goers (physically able), Slow Goers (not as active), No Goers (shut-ins, physically handicapped, advanced age); Golden Gaters; Golden Walnuts; J-O-Y Agers (Jesus and others and you); Jubilee Gems; Keenagers Club; Living Longer and Loving It; Prime Timers; Seasoned Saints; Senior Servants; Super Sixties (but they advertise 55 to 105!); The Golden Heirs (based on Romans 8:16 and 17); The Rejoicers; The Sunshine Bunch and Young at Heart.

Whatever name your group chooses, keep in mind your outreach to the unsaved. If you advertise group events to the community, you want a name that will convey to everyone the nature and purpose of your group.

---

[1]Win and Charles Arn, *Catch the Age Wave*, p. 75.

CHAPTER 6

Meetings

The senior group weekly or monthly meeting is the hub around which all the rest of the group activities will revolve. Pay close attention to it and make it a well-organized time of worship, fellowship, prayer and good times. Many churches make this meeting the main outreach arm of the group. Often unsaved friends of group members will attend a luncheon and a planned program with an interesting topic before they will attend a regular church service.

The majority of senior adult groups we interviewed meet once a month. Having a set day—the last Thursday of the month, for example—is the most convenient arrangement. It's easy to remember, and members can plan their calendars around it. The group usually meets at the church for a noon luncheon and a planned program. One group interviewed called this meeting their "Friendship Day."

Meetings during the day tend to attract older seniors since they are retired and free and often don't like to be out at night. However, groups sometimes meet in the evening or on Saturday in order to accommodate those who still have work schedules or other obligations during the day.

Some groups we interviewed meet twice a month, once for a luncheon/program and once for a work day. Some like to do impromptu things on their scheduled meeting date, depending on the weather. Others have six months of program meetings and six months of all-day trips. Another group takes three months off in the summer and three months off in the winter. The point is that there is no reason to feel tied down to any certain pattern. Meeting times and schedules are not sacred. Tailor the format to fit the needs of your group.

Where to meet? The majority of senior groups we interviewed meet in their church building. But if your church facilities are unavailable or inadequate, check out building options in your area. What about that nearby hospital? Make arrangements to eat lunch in its cafeteria and then use one of its conference rooms for your meeting. Other groups have used schools, libraries and village or town halls.

Format

The program should not concentrate on or emphasize the problems of senior adults, but rather it should encourage the seniors themselves. Like the rest of us, seniors need to be reassured. They need to know that God loves them and that the church values them enough to provide a program where they can get together with their peers for a time of fellowship and emotional and spiritual encouragement.

A suggested format for the program is the "Four S" formula: singing, a secular feature, a spiritual segment and a social element. Once you find the right pattern for your group, occasional surprise elements may help build interest, but keep the general pattern consistent.

It's also helpful to keep the program on a time schedule. Most people, even older people, have attention spans of less than one hour, so try to keep your program within this time frame. A great program can be presented effectively within 30 to 40 minutes. If you are planning a longer meeting or activity, let the group know ahead of time.

Plan programs with variety. Your senior adult meetings shouldn't be just another preaching service. It's easy to get stuck in a rut, but there are many different ways to get out of one. Here are some ideas our surveyed groups use to keep their programs fresh:

Music

• Center a music program around a theme. Put together several packages of music using your church members. Include as much variety as possible.

• Contact a special music group from an area church and let them present a concert.

• Choose music from a specific era, research it and play samples (use records or tapes if necessary). Many libraries provide music in CD or cassette form that can be checked out.

• Get some music that your group would recognize from earlier years and have a sing-along.

• Invite younger church members, even children, to give special music.

• Make sure everyone has an opportunity to take part in the program. Not only group singing but also special numbers by the musically gifted and the liberal use of volunteers help make people feel needed.

Devotions

• Base your devotions on a theme each month—stewardship or service, for example. One group we interviewed had devotionals on the different aspects of salvation.

• Give group members a chance to share short devotionals or testimonies.

• Have seniors share unique ways they've found to serve the Lord.

Games

• Board games, such as Scrabble or Monopoly, are popular activities for informal get-togethers.

• Active games, such as shuffleboard or horseshoes, can be used if you have the facilities.

• Team games are fun too. Use team names such as the Hatfields and McCoys, Confederates and Yankees, Farmers and City Slickers. One popular team game is "Show Me," in which each team is given a pile of newspapers. The game leader calls out articles such as "picture of a couch," "sports story" or "wedding announcement." The first team to tear out such an article scores. Bible quizzes or "sword drills" can be fit into the team format as well.

Some Suggestions

• Get an enthusiastic person to emcee the meetings, introduce and welcome guests, lead the singing and give the announcements. A happy spirit is contagious.

- Always include good humor.
- Recognize birthdays, anniversaries and announcements. Besides group announcements, give the seniors a chance to make personal announcements regarding births, anniversary celebrations and other events.
- If the group is large, provide name tags for each person.
- Have something fun for people to do as they arrive at the meeting, such as guessing how much candy is in a jar or putting together postcard puzzles (cut up postcards and mix them together).
- Include an occasional mixer so people don't get stuck with one group.

Special Speakers

Even though the gospel should be clearly presented at every senior group meeting, there is plenty of room within the program format for other topics—even those that don't have a spiritual theme. The key is to choose subjects that interest and benefit older adults. Discussion of secular topics that promote the intellectual development and physical well-being of your senior group are valid.

State and local agencies and public service organizations will often send out speakers to present their work to social and church groups. (Hint: if you have speakers who are not Christians, remember to give them guidelines about language and suitable subject matter.) The topics are endless, but the following is a list of some good ideas:

Health
- Blood pressure/cholesterol (Include a free blood pressure check; one group tried *regular* blood pressure checks, but they were unpopular since so many people have their own testing machines.)

- Eye care (Provide a free glaucoma check, if possible.)
- Nutrition
- Arthritis and rheumatism
- Hospital resources and information
- Long-term health-care costs
- Mental health

Safety
- CPR and first aid (American Red Cross)
- Gas/electricity in the home—conservation and safety suggestions
- Fire prevention
- Public safety
- Telephone concerns (dealing with threatening or obscene calls, available telephone hearing assistance)
- Weather (weather bureau speaker)

Miscellaneous
- Floral arranging
- Funeral preparations
- Library resources for senior adults
- Nonprofit organizations, such as the children's museum or local historical association
- Social Security
- Travel (Use travel films available from public libraries, or have someone in your church/group who has taken a trip share a "travelogue.")

Breaking Bread

Nothing warms people up like eating together, and your senior group can take full advantage of this sort of activity. Many seniors, especially those who live alone, look forward to eating with friends. Try alternating a few of the ideas below:

Traditional Potluck

Everyone brings food. People may sign up to bring certain dishes, or you may make assignments alphabetically. ("Last names beginning with A through M bring a salad and a main dish; last names beginning with N through Z bring a dessert and a main dish.") Provide the option of contributing money instead of food.

Alphabet Potluck

Have members bring a dish that begins with the first letter of their last name. For example: Adams—applesauce, avocado dip; Zimmerman—zwieback, zucchini. Have a sign-up sheet for people to indicate what type of dish they are bringing: main dish, salad, vegetable or dessert. Then you will know how to coordinate the meal.

Partial Potluck

Everyone brings a food item, but the main dish is provided out of group or church funds. Usually a freewill offering is given to cover the main dish expense. People bring either a salad or a dessert or an assigned item to supplement the meal, such as baked beans, cupcakes, Jell-O or pies. Vary the item each time.

Catered Meal

A catered meal once in a while is a fun and novel approach to the traditional potluck. There is a charge per person, but it usually is not exorbitant. A different slant on this is to have a group of volunteer members cater the meal. Appoint a kitchen "general" to plan the meal, order the food, coordinate the volunteers and maintain general supervision of the kitchen crew, including serving and cleaning up. Be creative, but don't overboard. Make appetizing meals with quality food, but keep them simple.

Food Themes

Another fun idea is to have food themes, such as salad day, ice cream sundae day, fish-fry day, barbecue day, or Oriental, Mexican or Italian day. Make a list of items needed for a theme meal and have everyone sign up to bring one item.

CHAPTER 7

Outreach

The need for evangelism within the senior community is immense. As previously noted, this is a rapidly growing age group with many needs. The senior adult group can reach these people in a way no one else can. Seniors usually respond best to the gospel when it is presented to them by people their own age, people with similar experiences. Instilling a desire for evangelism in the hearts of your senior group should be your highest goal.

Bringing Them In

Producing an effective outreach to unsaved seniors doesn't just happen—it takes forethought, as well as work. The following five elements can help assure that your senior group will maximize its outreach potential:

1. Have a well-planned program. Schedule your meetings at times convenient for older adults. Pay close attention to subject matter and choose relevant topics with interesting speakers. If the meetings are enjoyable, fun and worthwhile, the seniors will invite their friends, and their friends will be willing to attend.

2. Advertise! Seniors in the community won't know about your group if you don't get the word out. Announce group events and goings on in Sunday School and church—some of the younger people present may have older friends or relatives who would be interested. One group we surveyed checked newspapers for anniversary and retirement announcements for seniors in their community; then they sent those people an invitation to the group's next function. Submit news releases to local papers and radio stations if possible. Advertising of this sort must be long-term and targeted in order to see results.

3. Cultivate a spirit of caring and acceptance within your group. Nothing is so attractive to the unsaved as the love of God "shed abroad in our hearts" (Rom. 5:5). Nothing is so repulsive to them as a cold, uncaring spirit. If your group truly wishes to win people to Christ, it must overflow with love for others. Friendliness doesn't guarantee that people will trust Christ as Savior at your meetings, but without it they most assuredly won't.

4. Plan your meetings with the unsaved in mind. Always include a clear gospel presentation, even if the program is centered on a secular topic. This presentation can be some-

thing as simple as a testimony or a short devotional, but never ignore the gospel.

5. Make use of special outreach activities. Hold a Senior Seminar, for example, in which you bring in a special speaker on a topic of interest to seniors. Include a secular workshop (social services or medical services, for example), then have your group supply special music. Invite other churches if your group is too small to make such an event seem worthwhile.

One church we interviewed held a Senior Adult Fair. The group solicited the help of agencies that provide services for senior adults. Those agencies set up booths, and senior groups in the community were invited to come and tour.

Investigate the possibility of picking up people from nearby retirement homes for your group meetings. Some homes will even let you use one of their vehicles if some of their people are involved.

Visitation Ministry

Visitation is an important arm of your group's outreach ministry. Visitation may include calling on visitors, ill group members or fully shut-in persons with disabilities. Your visitation ministry should also include rest homes, hospitals, convalescent homes, retirement homes and rescue missions.

The nursing and retirement home ministry provides unique opportunities for seniors. It keeps them in contact with people who are older or in worse straits than they are, and it reminds them that ageism is a two-way street.

Setting up an effective nursing-home ministry should begin with the following steps:

• First, check with the home's activities director or administrator regarding visiting hours and proposed programs. Be sure you and your group are familiar with the home's rules.

• Hold your program at the same time every week or month—a hit-or-miss schedule will usually miss. If possible, have your programs included in the nursing home calendar.

• Keep the format short (30–45 minutes maximum), simple and centered on the gospel. The basic building blocks of your program should simply be special music, testimonies or a devotional and prayer. Once you have become more comfortable with this routine, move on to include more variety in your program: singing groups, puppets or sing-a-longs.

• In some situations, the more ambulatory residents appreciate being included in the service. Let them pass out songbooks, for instance, or be greeters.

• Remember to keep a personal touch. Include a time for your group members to have one-on-one contact with the residents—nearly all salvation decisions occur in this type of situation. Be a good listener. Read the Bible and pray with the patients. Also, ask the nursing personnel to recommend residents needing special attention. Visit the rooms of people who aren't able to come to the meetings. You may even consider taking the program to them!

PART FOUR

Senior Group
Events and Activities

Senior adults are like everybody else—they need diversion once in a while. They need fun and good times. You can keep the interest level of your group high by holding activities and events aside from the regular meetings.

Remember to give an activity more than one chance, especially if it's something new to your members. If those who tried it enjoy it, they'll spread the word. It's also helpful to announce the activity in the church service to attract seniors who don't attend the group meetings.

Concerning cost, it's beneficial to include a mix of activities—some free and some that cost. This variety gives everyone a chance to participate. You might even consider making scholarships available to those who can't afford activities.

CHAPTER 8

Special Events

The following are some examples of special events used by senior groups surveyed for this book.

• Meet in unusual places: on the church lawn, in back-yards, in picnic areas or in nursing homes (with patients participating).

• Plan a nostalgia day when the group members can share a memory using visuals/objects they bring in.

• Have an "Old Fashioned Day," when people dress

accordingly and bring foods such as what they had in their school lunches as children.

• Show a video on an interesting topic. Check your public library for possibilities.

• Have a drama presentation.

• Invite your church puppet team, if you have one, to present a program.

• Feature a "Favorite Recipe Day," when everyone brings a favorite recipe. That day is always popular.

• Have a treasure hunt.

• One group had success with a "Baby Picture Day," when everyone brought his baby picture.

• Hold a "Craft and Hobby Day." Each person brings a craft or hobby to exhibit. Have an emcee briefly interview each person about his or her craft or hobby.

• Try a talent hour. You'll be surprised what your group will come up with.

• Pack a picnic lunch and spend the day together at a nearby Bible conference.

• Plan a day program for the area fellowshipping churches, bring in a speaker and have a catered lunch. Take turns with the other churches in providing the program.

• Take a trip with a fellowshipping church's senior adult group. Going together will cut the cost and provide enjoyable fellowship.

• Dining out at a restaurant is always a favorite among seniors, especially after a Sunday church service or in conjunction with another activity. Smorgasbords or buffets are a favorite, but remember to be sensitive to your group's price range.

• Get together with senior adult groups from other fellowshipping churches. When your church has a Bible conference or other special event, send a special invitation to their senior adult groups inviting them to attend one of the meetings and to have dessert with your group afterward.

• Hold a special seminar to explore a relevant topic, such as caregiving, computers or travel.

• Try special meals, such as prayer breakfasts or progressive dinners. Use senior adults' homes or homes of volunteers from the congregation.

• One group we interviewed enjoyed holding a dinner cruise. Enjoy dinner aboard, and bring your own special music.

• Plan a senior-adult camp week and invite area fellowshipping churches.

• Try small recreational groups. If some members of your group enjoy a certain form of recreation—such as walking, bowling or golfing—begin a small group to do this activity together weekly.

• Initiate a walking program: Mark off your church parking lot to show different distances. Set a time for people to come and walk. Design a chart and let people fill in the distance they have walked. Work toward group total miles rather than competing individually.

• Have a quarterly birthday party celebrating the birth of group members who had birthdays within that time period.

• Hold Christmas and Valentine banquets. Pick couples to serve as the host and hostess of their own table. Prior to the banquet, the couples can invite others to sit at their table. They also decorate their table and bring their own table settings (may be crystal and china or paper plates). Make sure everyone is included. Widows, widowers and other seniors who otherwise may not come because they feel uncomfortable sitting alone may be willing to attend this kind of banquet.

• Plan a Senior Sunday or Grandparent's Day. Most

churches celebrate Senior Sunday on Grandparent's Day. Some plan a week of activities for the seniors. Even if this approach won't work for your group, always try to make Senior Sunday special. Have special seating for your seniors, for instance. Or honor them in some way: give them boutonnieres and small corsages or small devotional books; have church members invite seniors to their homes for Sunday dinner (make sure everyone gets an invitation), or have a special Sunday dinner for the seniors in the church fellowship hall.

Involving your seniors in the service on Senior Sunday is a good idea. They can serve as ushers, give the announcements, share testimonies and perform special music (even a cantata if you have enough members). One may even be qualified to preach the sermon.

CHAPTER 9

Trips

Ask many seniors what their favorite group activity is, and they'll respond, "Going on trips!" Whether it's for an hour or a week, the trip is a fun and rewarding activity for senior groups.

Short Trips

Short trips last for only a day or an afternoon. They're popular with seniors because they don't have to plan or pack for being away overnight, and the costs are fairly low.

Ideas for day trip destinations are many. Evaluate a prospective destination by asking these questions: Is it interesting? Is it educational? Is it fun? If the destination includes these three elements, it will most likely be an enjoyable day trip.

The destination can, but need not be, spiritual in nature. The object of the group trip is to provide a fun way for your group members to get to know each other, to fellowship together, and to bring in their unsaved friends. If necessary, a short devotional time can follow or precede the trip.

If you're having trouble coming up with places to go on the short trip, chances are you're neglecting things close to home. It's the can't-see-the-forest-for-the-trees syndrome. There are likely many fascinating places nearby that you have never noticed or considered.

Here are some short-trip destinations senior adult groups have enjoyed. Many of these destinations provide group tours.

- Amish country
- Museum: art, historical, nature
- Botanical garden
- Christian publisher
- Children's home
- Color tour or "back roads" excursion
- College or seminary
- Craft fair
- City festivals (apple festival, tulip festival and so on)
- Fruit orchard
- Nursery or garden center
- Historical monument
- Planetarium
- Parade of Homes tour
- Bible conference

- Nature preserve
- Restored antique home
- Park
- Presidential library
- Professional sporting event
- Shopping expedition
- Zoo

Long Trips

Most senior groups *love* long trips—trips of three to five days are the most popular. Seniors say they enjoy the longer trips since it gives them a chance to take a vacation they probably wouldn't take otherwise. On a group-sponsored getaway, they don't have to worry about driving, car maintenance, directions or accommodation details.

Long trips aren't frivolous fun—they have proved to be extremely effective outreach tools. Unsaved seniors are often willing to go on these trips because they see them as non-threatening; they don't fear that they'll be constantly pressured to make a spiritual decision. And after they get to know some of the group members and begin to feel more comfortable, they'll usually be willing to attend other church or group functions. Besides, the long trip provides the unsaved a unique opportunity to observe the Christian way of life in action.

The following are some suggested destinations for long trips:

- Mall of America, Skydome
- Natural attractions, such as the Black Hills, Niagara Falls, the Grand Canyon, the Great Lakes
- Parks and wildlife areas: Acadia, Hot Springs, Petrified Forest, Voyageurs, Yosemite (to name just a few)
- Tourist attraction areas

- Bible conferences
- Fall or spring color tours

The long trip is an ambitious endeavor, and it requires much long-range planning and organization. You will need to prearrange motel accommodations, arrival and departure times, bus routes, cost per person and restaurant arrangements. So you'll need someone with a gift for organization to be in charge. But most senior groups that have tried the long trip have found it to be more than worth the extra effort. If your group would like to try its hand at the long trip, see Appendixes C and D (pp. 79–93) for some valuable planning information and forms to photocopy and use.

CHAPTER 10

Projects

Older people don't like to feel unproductive, but they often do, since they've retired and their families have moved out of the house. The special project helps seniors battle this notion by providing them with an outlet for their energy, creativity and abilities. At the same time, the project is a means for your group members to serve Christ by giving of themselves for the good of others. (If the regular senior adult group is designed solely for outreach, the projects could be performed by the senior Sunday School class.)

Try these service ideas:

"Fix It Club" or "Worker's Group." Such organizations assist the ill, widows and needy with maintenance, cleaning and other practical needs. Both men and women contribute their skills in this type of a project. If it is a household repair or construction type project, the women can help as needed or cook a meal for the working men. This is a good way for the younger seniors to be of use to the older group members.

Service Projects. Plan a yearly service project. Most Christian ministries (Shepherds Baptist Ministries, Baptist Children's Home, Michigan Christian Home and many Christian camps, to name a few) depend heavily on the helping hands of volunteers. Most of these organizations have multitudes of tasks that a group of older people can perform. Your group may be able to spend an hour or two, a day or even a week serving one of these organizations. Your senior adults will be excited to see that their efforts can, indeed, make a difference.

Provide an orientation program, if necessary, to help your people serve the chosen organization more effectively. Be sure to plan the details carefully, including meal arrangements and accommodations, in order not to be a burden to the ministry you are helping.

If your group is small, try combining your efforts with those of another local fellowshipping senior group on an evangelism program, a nursing home ministry or special services.

Telephone Ministry. Enlist a group of people, each of whom is assigned to specific shut-ins. The volunteers call their assigned shut-ins regularly, at an agreed-on time. The shut-ins gain a sense of security from knowing that someone is watching out for them and that they have someone to call on if they have a need.

Adopt-a-Shut-In. This is similar to the phone ministry, but on a more personal level. Individual senior adults adopt a shut-in. They visit the person and keep in phone contact with him or her, and may even give a regular report to the group, detailing how their adopted shut-in is doing. End the project or rotate adoptees every six months to prevent the ministry from becoming a burden.

Transportation Committee. This group provides transportation to church, Sunday School or senior group meetings for those who need it.

Christmas and Thanksgiving Baskets. The women bake their "specialties," and the men provide fruit and nuts. Have a get-together to make up the baskets and then deliver them to the needy or shut-ins.

School Assistance. Offer your group's services to your church-affiliated school, if one exists, or to other Christian schools in the area. A senior group that performs some service in a public school has a unique way of representing Christ in the community.

Care Packages. Make and send "care packages" of baked goods, treats, devotional books, or other needed items for church members who are college students or in the armed services.

Home Visits. Visit homes for the mentally or physically disabled. Read, play games or just talk with the residents. They crave (and need) such attention.

Tutoring. Tutor children in the church who need help with schoolwork.

Ladies' Group. Put together a ladies' group to assist in missions' sewing projects, quilting for service ministries and beautifying the church by decorating, painting, sewing curtains or cleaning.

Letter-Writing. Write letters to missionaries. This is a much-needed ministry in any church. Shut-ins especially may enjoy this task, for it's a way they can contribute.

Gift Showers. Conduct food or paper-product showers for Christian organizations or needy individuals.

Book Supply. Purchase, package and mail Bibles or Christian books to other countries.

CHAPTER 11

The Senior
Newsletter

Many senior groups thoroughly enjoy publishing their own newsletter, detailing what's going on in their circles. This paper is usually circulated among group members or even the church body at large. The senior newsletter is not just for the larger groups, though; even smaller churches can usually dig up enough news about themselves and their group to fill a single-sheet publication.

Let the group members themselves, if they wish, do the

news gathering, writing, publishing and distributing. If desired, someone else in the church with editorial or publishing experience may get involved, but you don't necessarily need a staff of correspondents and copy editors to produce a quality paper. All it takes is a little attention to detail. Try hard to keep the paper free from typos and misspelled words, especially if the newsletter is to be distributed in the community. Sloppy work gives the cause of Christ—and your group—a bad name.

The paper should focus on the group and its people. Tell what's going on in the group: activities, projects, schedules, itineraries, and so on. List people news, such as birthdays, anniversaries, prayer requests and answers to prayer.

Here are some other ideas to include in the paper:

• Senior of the Week. Publish an interview of a "senior of the week" and his or her background, job, family, hobbies, and so on. This feature helps the group members get to know one another, especially if the group is large. A variation of this feature is to interview a group member after one of the group's activities and poll his or her reaction to the event. This interview can be a real plug for your group and may coax others into trying the activity next time.

• Guess Who. Include a picture of one of the members when he or she was younger, together with the caption "Can you guess who this is?" Give the answer in the next issue.

• Devotionals

• Guest Columnist. A guest column can be written by alternating people: the pastor, the youth pastor, the senior-adult group leader or Sunday School teacher.

• Recipes

• Word games, quizzes and puzzles

• Poems

• Cartoons, jokes, funny sayings

- Grandchildren quotes
- Local history tidbits
- Short fiction pieces
- Health tips
- "How-to" articles
- Senior group meeting schedule
- Church office hours and phone number
- Service agencies' names and phone numbers

Conclusion

Goal-setting, leadership, research, planning, coordination, enthusiasm, caring, outreach, prayer—all are ingredients of a vigorous senior ministry. Your church can have one if it is willing—willing to make the effort necessary, willing to look beyond social stigmas and preconceived notions, and willing to see the needs *and* the abilities of this booming population.

Appendixes

Appendixes B through D were derived from material shared by Blackhawk Baptist Church, Fort Wayne, Indiana.

Suggested Reading

Roger L. Hauser. *Activities with Senior Adults*. Nashville: Broadman Press, 1987.

W. L. Howse III, compiler. *Senior Adult Leader's Notebook*. Nashville: Convention Press, 1990.

Horace L. Kerr. *How to Minister to Senior Adults in Your Church*. Nashville: Broadman Press, 1980.

Bob Sessoms. *150 Ideas for Activities with Senior Adults*. Nashville: Broadman Press, 1977.

Earl and Ruth Stallings. *Seniors Reaching Seniors*. Nashville: Convention Press, n.d.

Win Arn has books, study courses, tapes and newsletters dealing with senior adults. Order from:

L.I.F.E. International
1921 South Myrtle Avenue
Monrovia, CA 91016
1-800-423-4844

Sample Meeting Checklist

PROGRAM
❏ speaker
❏ special music
❏ pianist
❏ greeters
❏ other participants

FOOD
❏ remind people what to bring
❏ napkins
❏ plastic tableware
❏ plates, bowls, cups, tablecloths
❏ pitchers for cold drinks
❏ urn for hot water
❏ coffee, tea, cream, sugar, iced tea, other beverages
❏ kitchen crew organized

ROOM SETUP
❏ piano
❏ serving tables
❏ eating tables and chairs
❏ literature display
❏ sound system and hearing aids
❏ speaker needs, such as a projector
❏ extension cord, screen
❏ podium
❏ check room temperature
❏ hymnbooks or songsheets
❏ name tags and pins

ANNOUNCEMENTS
❏ sick
❏ prayer requests and praises
❏ birthdays and anniversaries
❏ future meetings and activities
❏ nursing home programs
❏ personal announcements

TRANSPORTATION
❏ confirm bus drivers
❏ distribute bus routes and keys
❏ load wheelchair if needed

Planning the Long Trip

I. General Investigation
A. Write the Chamber of Commerce in cities of interest and ask for maps, restaurant and motel lists and sightseeing brochures.
B. Ask friends and group members for information and brochures from places they have visited in their personal travels.
C. File gathered material in file folders by cities or states.
D. Include as many interests as possible within one trip.

II. Specific Investigation
A. Determine the major cities or points you wish to see. Write the appropriate Chamber of Commerce if you need additional planning information.
B. Obtain motel rates. You can often get a good price on private motels, but they should be checked out in person. (Some leaders actually take the planned trip first, staying in the motels and eating in the restaurants to be sure everything is acceptable.)
C. Determine approximate round-trip mileage. (Keep daily travel to 300 miles.)
D. Learn about availability, approximate price per mile or package price of bus lines.

III. Accommodations

A. Determine approximately how many rooms will be needed in the following categories:
   1. Two to a room: one bed
   2. Two to a room: two beds
   3. Three to a room: two beds
   4. Four to a room: two beds

B. Negotiate with a motel for group rates for each of the above categories. Make sure tax is included. Ask the following questions:
   1. Is a free room offered for the host and hostess? for the bus driver?
   2. Are all rooms air-conditioned? Do they have televisions? Are soda machines and ice available? If so, are there additional charges for these amenities?
   3. What is the deposit required to hold the rooms? When is it due?
   4. Will the motel assign rooms in one area so your group can be together?
   5. Will the motel prepare individual room keys for the group before your arrival if you send them a room list?
   6. How close is the bus discharge point to the rooms?
   7. What are nearest restaurants' price ranges and hours of operation? (It is desirable to have a reasonably priced restaurant within walking distance of the motel.)

C. Confirm by letter your understanding of all arrangements, especially the rates and approximate number of rooms, and request a letter from the motel confirming those details.

IV. Tour Arrangements

A. Write to all points of interest, advising them of your approximate group number and of the date you are thinking of visiting them. Ask them for the following:

1. Brochures describing their facilities
2. Information about on-site or nearby restaurants or snack bars
3. Hours of operation and length of time recommended to see everything
4. Group rates, including minimum number required and age requirements
5. Availability and rental cost of wheelchairs, if appropriate for your group
6. Any bus parking fees or restrictions.

B. Evaluate all tour data and formulate a daily schedule (see Appendix D, Form #1).

V. Bus Arrangements

A. Calculate round-trip mileage.

B. Add the miles that you will need for visiting points of interest.

C. Add about 50 miles a day as a cushion for diverting to restaurants, unplanned attractions, and so forth.

D. Call the bus company you have chosen and tell them your plans. Let them know the room arrangements you have negotiated for the bus driver. Ask them the following:

1. Who pays for the bus driver's meals?
2. Are parking fees, tolls, permits for special areas and all driver's expenses included in the price?
3. What extra costs can you expect?
4. Is there an extra charge if your mileage estimate

turns out to be low?

5. Is there a mileage/hours limit on how long the bus driver can operate each day?
6. Are there any luggage restrictions?
7. Is the bus air-conditioned?
8. Does the bus have adequate rest rooms?

E. Finalize your plans with the bus company, make necessary changes in schedules, and get written confirmation of your agreement.

VI. Final Tour Arrangements

A. Write to the points of interest you have scheduled, advising them of the following (be sure to keep a copy of each letter):
1. Date and time of arrival
2. Group rate you expect to pay at time of arrival and approximate number in the group
3. Amount of time you have allowed to see their facility
4. Wheelchair reservations, if needed
5. Restaurant reservations, if you are eating in their restaurant

VII. Total Trip Cost (Trip costs usually divide into fixed expenses [nonrefundable expenses] and adjustable expenses [expenses such as motels and tours that can be altered slightly to fit the group]).

A. Add up the fixed costs (see Appendix D, Form #2).
B. Set the minimum number of participants you need to keep the cost reasonable. Divide the total fixed cost by the minimum number of participants to get the fixed cost per person. (Six to eight persons fewer than the bus seating capacity is a good figure.)

C. Set the sign-up date at least four to six weeks prior to the departure date. If the minimum number of participants fails to sign up, plan to cancel the trip.

D. Add up the cost of the tour per person.

E. Determine individual motel cost (see Appendix D, Form #3).

F. Add the fixed cost, motel cost and tour cost for each individual to determine his/her total trip cost.

G. Round the totals to the nearest full dollar upward for ease in collecting money.

H. Request a $10 to $15 nonrefundable deposit upon signing up for the trip. This deposit will encourage firm decisions and will decrease cancellations.

I. Set up a payment schedule, keeping in mind that Social Security checks are scheduled for delivery on the third of each month. Try to keep monthly payments around $20 to $25. (Asking for one large sum discourages many.)

VIII. Publicity

A. Prepare a trip brochure, including the following items:

1. Dates, including the number of days and nights
2. Age limit
3. Points of interest scheduled
4. Names and phone numbers of motels
5. Payment schedule and deadline (Make the deadline at least two weeks prior to departure date.)
6. Minimum number of participants required to cover expenses (Explain that the trip will be canceled and money refunded if this minimum is not met.)

7. Policies about drinking, tobacco and dress (Often the unsaved participate in trips.)
8. Meal arrangements (Meals are extra personal expenses.)
9. Prices for various motel room combinations (example: two per room, one bed—$ _____)
10. Name of person to whom money should be paid.

B. Explain your policies:
1. Priority policy. "We give members of our senior adult group first priority for trip sign-ups. Second priority goes to new local folks and third priority to out-of-towners."
2. Traveling policy. "Everyone must stay with the group. The trip route cannot be diverted for special drop-offs to relatives or friends. If you wish to meet relatives or friends, you must make arrangements to meet with them at our motel."
3. Seating policy. "Travelers must change bus seats at least once a day in order to enhance fellowship and provide fair seating for all." (This policy eliminates the scramble for the front seat the first day and minimizes grumbling about having to ride over the wheels or near the back.)

C. Include a form to be turned in with the first payment (see Appendix D, Form #4). You may need some of this information to settle priority questions if you have a waiting list. It may also be helpful in case of an emergency during the trip.

D. Publicize the trip.
1. Announce in church, Sunday School, your senior adult meetings, your senior adult paper, the local newspaper and the community news bulletin on radio and TV.

2. Make posters for your church foyer and senior adult bulletin board.

IX. Money Collection

A. Appoint someone to collect the money and maintain a list of trip participants.

B. Follow up monthly on the payment schedule to keep everyone current.

C. Put together the room combinations as people sign up.

X. Final Plans

A. Mail in the motel room deposits six to eight weeks prior to your departure. Mail the balance due, less $50, two weeks prior to your departure. Most motels will not accept personal checks but will accept group or church checks *in advance*. Most will accept VISA and MasterCard credit cards. (Using a credit card minimizes the money you have to carry.)

B. Finalize tourist attraction arrangements. (Some tourist attractions require you to advise them in writing in advance in order to be eligible for group rates.) Try not to pay in advance for tourist attractions, because people may get sick or tired and not want to tour a particular attraction.

C. Mail a room list to all motels about one week before leaving (see Appendix D, Form #5).

D. Work out ride arrangements to and from the bus departure site for your trip. Be sure to let transportation volunteers know what time you will be returning.

E. Gather supplies to take on the bus:
1. Water coolers for drinking water (Refill each day.)
2. Cups, napkins, trash bags

3. Soft drinks (Cool drinks are always welcome, especially when there's a traffic jam, when the bus breaks down or when meals are a little late. Consider using a clean garbage can to keep soft drinks in. Every morning you can fill it with ice from the motel.)
4. Tracts and evangelistic handouts
5. Reading material to pass around the bus
6. Portable public address system (if necessary)
7. Additional trip guidelines and itinerary
8. Forms with emergency medical data *(Crucial!)*
9. A road atlas

F. Be sure you have the following items with you:
1. Copies of all motel and tourist attraction confirmation letters
2. Appropriate city maps
3. Directions to all planned tourist attractions
4. Motel and restaurant listings for each area you are visiting

G. Determine how much money you need to take in cash or traveler's checks (Carry this money with you.)
1. Balance of motel costs (Bring along proof of payments you have already made.)
2. Tourist attraction costs
3. Anticipated pay-phone-call expenses
4. Food expenses for you and your spouse
5. Potential taxi expense to return sick tourists to motel
6. Anticipated parking fees, permits or tolls not being paid by bus driver
7. Personal money for souvenirs and other personal expenses

8. At least $200 for the unexpected (If you have planned properly, this money should never be needed. Bus drivers often carry large cash advances and could possibly lend you something with permission from the company. But it is better to be safe than to sit at Western Union waiting for someone to wire you money.)

XI. Bus Guidelines

A. Require that all baggage be assembled for loading 30 minutes prior to final departures from motels.

B. Restrict travelers to two bags each and enforce any luggage restrictions the bus company has.

C. Always be the last one boarding the bus and the first one off so you can do the following:

   1. Assist people on and off the bus. (Be at the bus 15 minutes prior to the expected boarding time.)

   2. Provide a box for an extra step between the first bus step and the ground.

   3. Take a head count when loading and unloading the bus.

D. Put tracts on bus seats each morning and encourage your group to distribute them throughout the day. Also give out itineraries as needed.

E. Conduct a devotional time on the bus each morning before leaving the motel. (This time may include a group hymn, prayer and a brief devotion or Scripture reading.)

F. Change seats once a day. Have everyone on the right side move back one seat and everyone on the left side move forward one seat.

G. Announce where and when the group should reassemble before anyone gets off the bus. Explain the tourist attraction times and locations. Make clear that anyone afraid of getting lost or needing assistance may stay with you. Tell your group members what to do if they should get lost.

XII. Motel Stops

A. Go to the motel office while a few men disembark to assist the bus driver in unloading the luggage.

B. Copy room numbers so you have a ready list of the room assignments.

C. Assign a room captain for each room and hand out room keys while your group is still on the bus. Let the group members know your room number and tell them to bring any problems or complaints to you.

D. Help your group members carry their luggage to their rooms.

E. Call each of the rooms to be sure everyone is settled and all is well.

APPENDIX D
Forms

Form 1
DAILY SCHEDULE FOR THE LONG TRIP

Schedule for _____
(date)

	Time
Meet for breakfast	_____
Load buses	_____
Arrival times for morning tourist attractions	
Attraction #1	_____
Attraction #2	_____
Lunch	_____
(Consider 11:30 A.M. or 1:00 P.M. to avoid crowds.)	
Arrival times for afternoon tourist attractions	
Attraction #1	_____
Attraction #2	_____
Evening meal	_____
(It is advisable to return to the motel to clean up, rest and then walk to dinner. If driving, try to eat around 4:30–5:00 P.M. or after 6:30 P.M. to avoid crowds.)	
Evening activities	
Activity #1	_____
Activity #2	_____

Form 2
LONG TRIP FIXED COSTS

Bus . . . . _____

Estimated tolls and parking fees . . . . _____

Telephone calls to make arrangements . . . . _____

Pay phone calls while on tour . . . . _____

Printing and mailing costs . . . . _____

Correspondence costs . . . . _____

Meals for host (include tips) . . . . _____

Motel costs, if any, for host . . . . _____

Taxi fares to return sick tourists to motel . . _____

Other fixed costs . . . . _____

Cushion per person . . . . _____

TOTAL . . . . _____

Form 3
LONG TRIP MOTEL COSTS

Name _____

Trip _____

	MOTEL	2 per room 1 bed	2 per room 2 beds	3 per room 2 beds	4 per room 2 beds
Night 1					
Night 2					
Night 3					
Night 4					
Night 5					

Total motel cost. . . . . _____

Fixed cost per person. _____

Tour cost per person . . . . _____

TOTAL . . . . _____

LONG TRIP PARTICIPANT FORM

Name _____

Address _____

City _____ State _____ Zip _____

Date form received: _____

Preferred motel arrangements: _____

_____

Number per room: _____

Number per bed: _____

Roommate requested: _____

Amount of nonrefundable deposit required: _____

Doctor's name and phone number: _____

_____

Prescriptions you are currently taking: _____

_____

Medical conditions: _____

_____

Allergies: _____

In case of emergency, contact: _____

SAMPLE LONG TRIP MOTEL LETTER

July 10
ABC Motel
Anywhere, USA

Dear Manager:

In order to facilitate our group's arrival, we are sending you the following list with names and group room assignments. The groups listed inside quotation marks ("/") prefer first-floor rooms.

Please assign rooms as close together as possible. The deposit was mailed _____, and we will complete payment upon our arrival. It would be helpful if room keys could be prepared before our arrival with individual names assigned. Thank you for your help. We look forward to staying with you.

Please contact _____ at _____ if you have any questions or if we can be of further help.

	Names	Room Type
Group 1	_____	_____
Group 2	_____	_____
Group 3	_____	_____
Group 4	_____	_____
Group 5	_____	_____
Group 6	_____	_____
Group 7	_____	_____
Group 8	_____	_____
Group 9	_____	_____
Group 10	_____	_____

Bibliography

Arn, Win and Charles. *Catch the Age Wave.* Grand Rapids: Baker Book House, 1993.

_____. *The New Senior.* Monrovia, CA: L.I.F.E. International, 1993.

Cheney, Walter J., William J. Diehm and Franke Seeley. *The Second Fifty Years.* New York: Paragon House, 1992.

Hauser, Roger L. *Activities with Senior Adults.* Nashville: Broadman Press, 1987.

Howse III, W. L., compiler. *Senior Adult Leader's Notebook.* Nashville: Convention Press, 1990.

Kerr, Horace L. *How to Minister to Senior Adults in Your Church.* Nashville: Broadman Press, 1980.

Lampman, George. *The "Super Sixties" of Blackhawk. Senior Adults: An Untapped Resource.* Fort Wayne, IN: Blackhawk Baptist Church, n.d.

Metropolitan Life Insurance Co. *The Statistical Bulletin*, Vol. 74, No. 3, July–September 1993.

Sell, Charles M. *Transition: The Stages of Adult Life.* Chicago: Moody Press, 1985.

Sessoms, Bob. *150 Ideas for Activities with Senior Adults.* Nashville: Broadman Press, 1977.

Stallings, Earl and Ruth Stallings. *Seniors Reaching Seniors.* Nashville: Convention Press, n.d.

U.S. Bureau of the Census. *Current Population Reports, Series P-25, No. 1092.* "Population projections of the U.S. by age, sex, race, and Hispanic origin: 1992 to 2050." Washington, D.C., November 1992.